AF614924

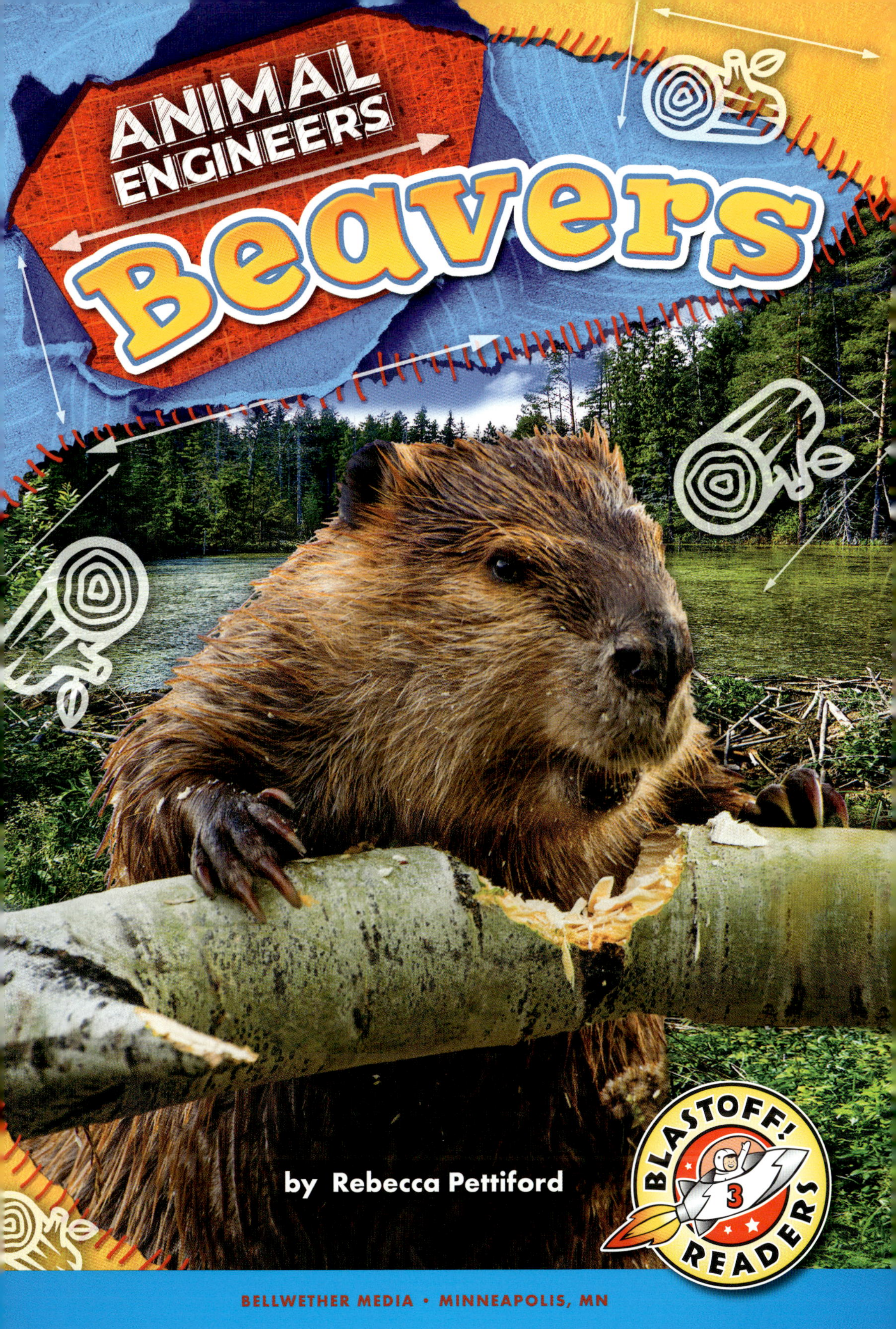
ANIMAL ENGINEERS
Beavers
by Rebecca Pettiford
BLASTOFF! 3 READERS
BELLWETHER MEDIA • MINNEAPOLIS, MN

Blastoff! Readers are carefully developed by literacy experts to build reading stamina and move students toward fluency by combining standards-based content with developmentally appropriate text.

Level 1 provides the most support through repetition of high-frequency words, light text, predictable sentence patterns, and strong visual support.

Level 2 offers early readers a bit more challenge through varied sentences, increased text load, and text-supportive special features.

Level 3 advances early-fluent readers toward fluency through increased text load, less reliance on photos, advancing concepts, longer sentences, and more complex special features.

★ **Blastoff! Universe**

Reading Level

Grade K

Grades 1–3

Grade 4

This edition first published in 2025 by Bellwether Media, Inc.

Library of Congress Cataloging-in-Publication Data

LC record for Beavers available at: https://lccn.loc.gov/2024015039

Editor: Rachael Barnes Designer: Josh Brink

Printed in the United States of America, North Mankato, MN.

Table of Contents

Busy Builders

Beavers are large **rodents**. These **mammals** build dams to stop flowing water. This raises the water level and forms ponds.

The water keeps beavers safe from **predators**. Beavers also build **lodges** in these ponds.

lodge

There are two beaver **species**. North American beavers live in much of North America. Eurasian beavers live in parts of Europe and Asia.

Eurasian beaver

Beavers live in rivers, streams, and lakes. They also spend time on land.

Planning Dams and Lodges

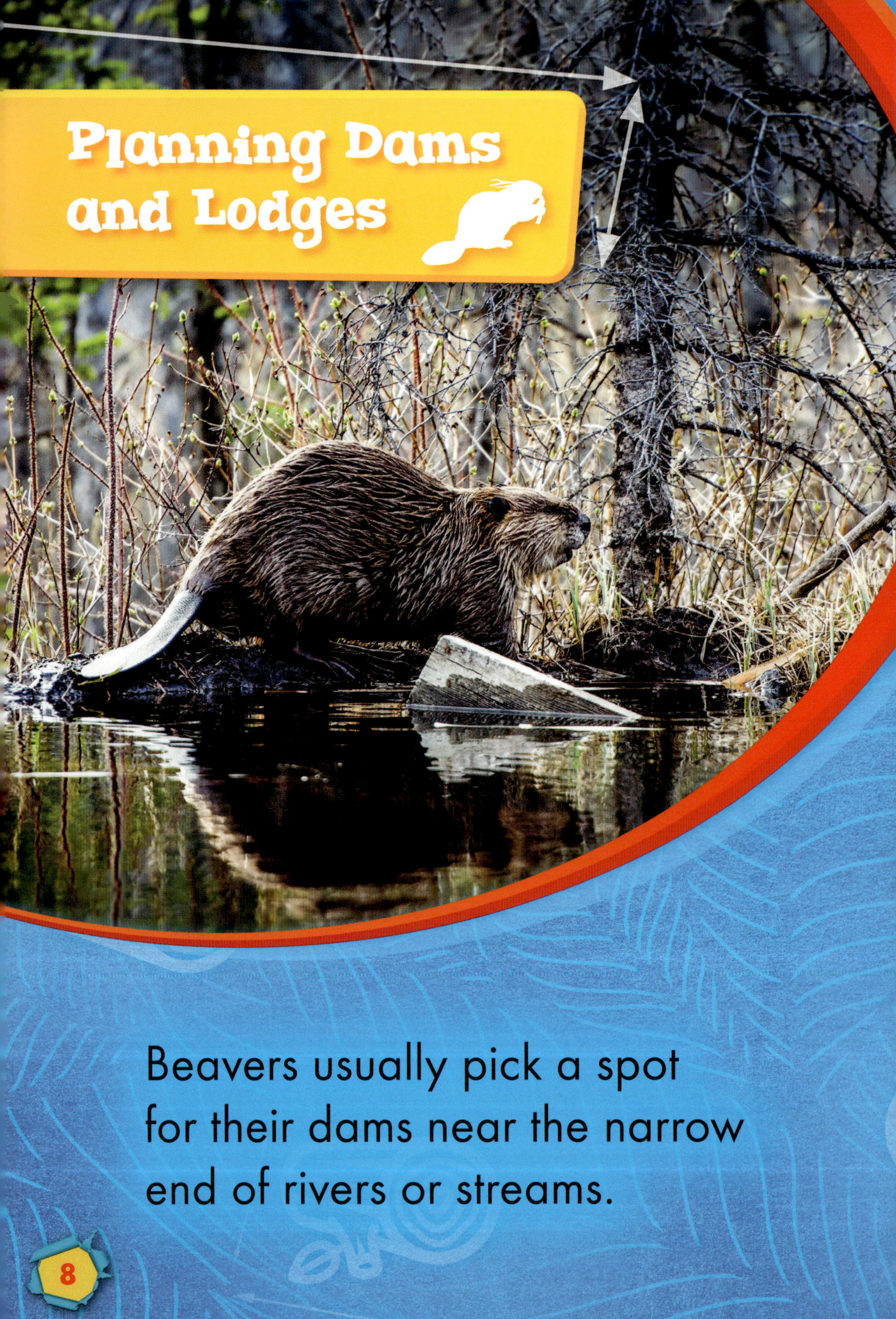

Beavers usually pick a spot for their dams near the narrow end of rivers or streams.

They build dams
near wooded areas.
These **habitats** have
rocks and trees for building.

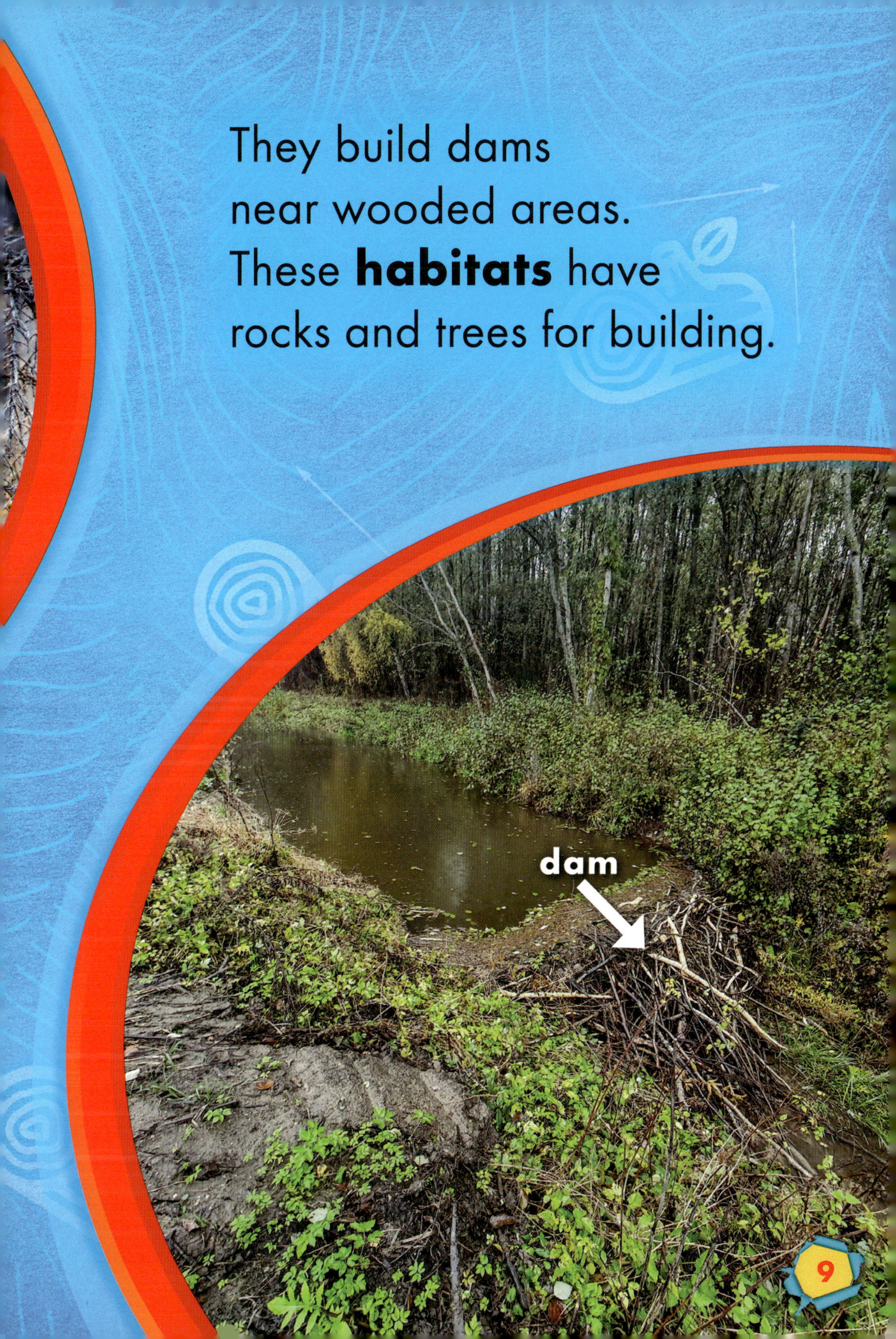

Beavers build dams year-round. They slow down during the winter.

They build lodges near dams. Beavers work on their dams and lodges as long as they live in the pond.

Beavers are mostly active at night. They come onto land and use their large **incisors** to gnaw through trees.

Beavers use their mouths to drag branches to water. They move them to the work area.

Beavers use their front paws to carry rocks to the dam. Some rocks keep branches in place.

Then beavers add mud to **seal** the dam. Beaver families work together to build dams!

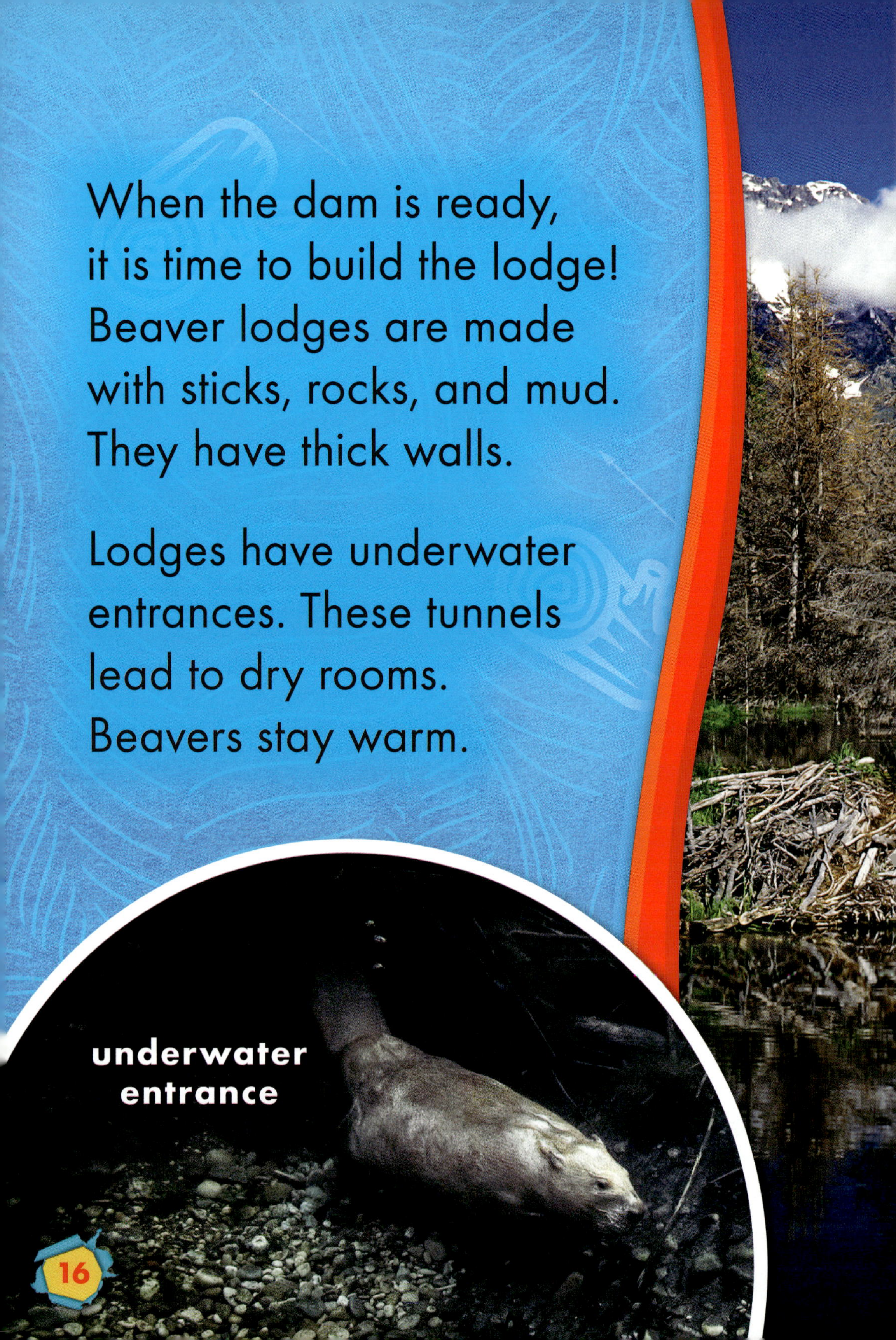

When the dam is ready, it is time to build the lodge! Beaver lodges are made with sticks, rocks, and mud. They have thick walls.

Lodges have underwater entrances. These tunnels lead to dry rooms. Beavers stay warm.

underwater entrance

lodge
dam

The Dam and Lodge Are Ready!

Dams force water to spread out. This creates new **wetlands**. Many animals make homes in them!

Beavers use deeper parts of the wetlands to store food underwater for the winter.

Identify Beaver Dams and Lodges

- look for ponds with large structures built from rocks, branches, and mud
- dams are wider, lodges are taller

Beavers may leave their pond if **threatened** by predators or if food runs out. Deserted dams start to leak. The pond **drains**.

draining dam

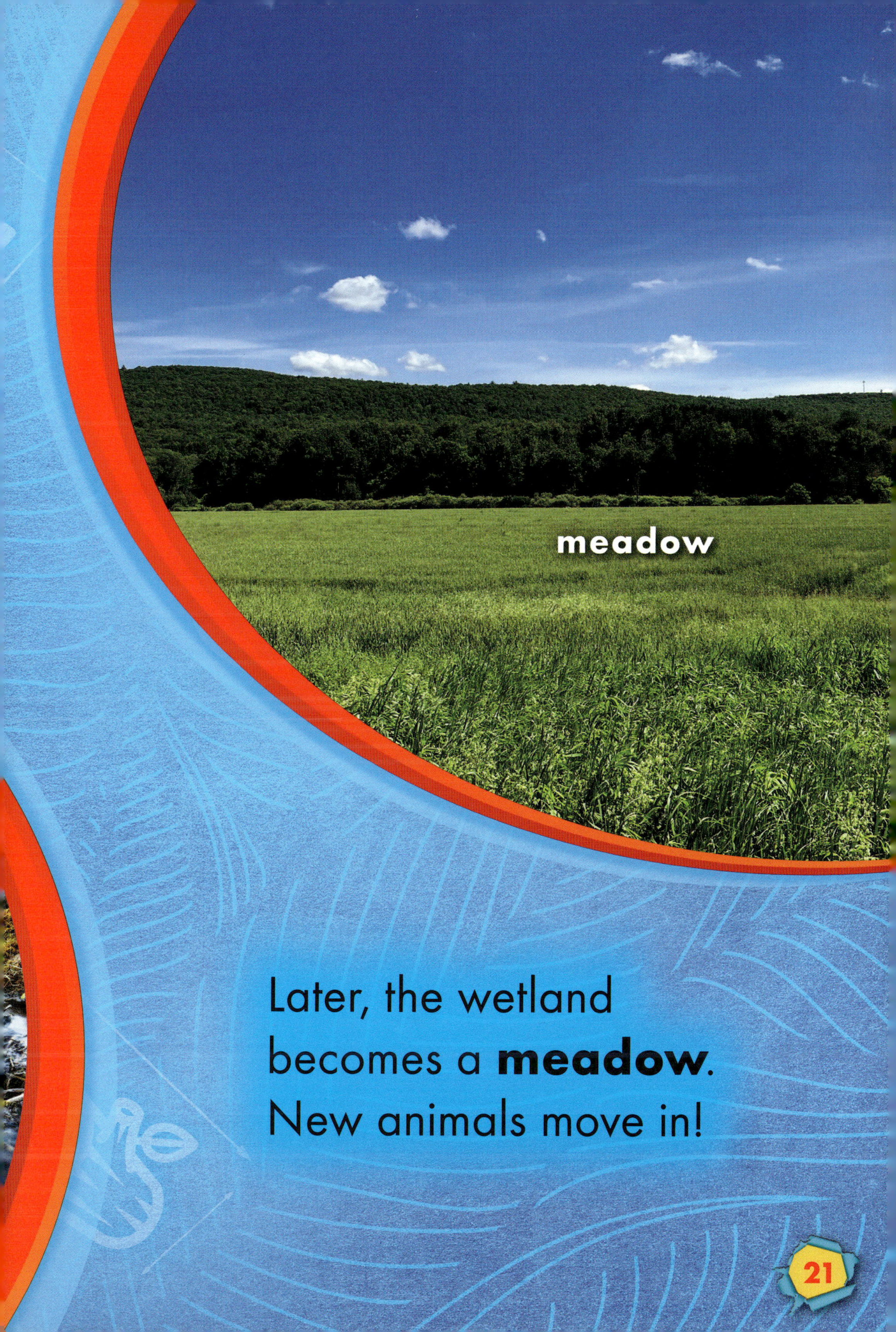

Later, the wetland becomes a **meadow**. New animals move in!

Glossary

drains–slowly loses water from an area

habitats–the natural homes of plants and animals

incisors–sharp teeth at the front of the mouth for cutting food

lodges–shelters beavers build in water made of branches and mud

mammals–warm-blooded animals that have backbones and feed their young milk

meadow–a field of grass

predators–animals that hunt other animals for food

rodents–small animals that gnaw on their food

seal–to close off to keep water from going through

species–kinds of animals

threatened–in danger

wetlands–areas of land that are covered with low levels of water for most of the year

To Learn More

AT THE LIBRARY

Chanez, Katie. *Beaver Kits in the Wild.* Minneapolis, Minn.: Jump!, 2024.

Furstinger, Nancy. *Beaver Dams.* New York, N.Y.: AV2 by Weigel, 2020.

Riggs, Kate. *Beavers.* Mankato, Minn.: The Creative Company, 2023.

ON THE WEB

FACTSURFER

Factsurfer.com gives you a safe, fun way to find more information.

1. Go to www.factsurfer.com.

2. Enter "beavers" into the search box and click 🔍.

3. Select your book cover to see a list of related content.

Index

The images in this book are reproduced through the courtesy of: Danita Delimont, cover (hero beaver); SGeneralov, cover (background dam); milehightraveler, p. 3 (TOC); Vladimir Turkenich, p. 4; Adam Welz/ Alamy, p. 5; Podolnaya Elena, p. 6; Ghost Bear, pp. 8-9, 23; GiedriusLT, p. 9; bieszczady_wildlife, p. 10; lussiya, p. 11; stanley45, pp. 12-13; Christian Musat, p. 13; Robert McGouey/ Wildlife/ Alamy, p. 13 (incisors); Rosanne Tackaberry/ Alamy, pp. 14-15; Ronnie Howard, p. 15 (branches); Rejean Aline Bedard, pp. 15 (mud), 19 (tunnel); Jeff Foott/ Getty, p. 15 (rocks); SuperStock/ Ingo Arndt/ Minden Pictures, pp. 16, 19 (lodge); Clement Philippe/ Alamy, pp. 16-17; Ross Knowlton Nature Photography/ Alamy, p. 18; Nicole_N, pp. 18-19 (background and dam); David Fossler, pp. 18-19 (beaver den); Brent Beach/ Alamy, pp. 20-21; Verysmallplanet, p. 21.